GOOD LUCK

GOOD LUCK

Anna Livesey

Victoria University Press

VICTORIA UNIVERSITY PRESS
Victoria University of Wellington
PO Box 600 Wellington

Copyright © Anna Livesey 2003

ISBN 0 86473 459 X

First published 2003

National Library of New Zealand Cataloguing-in-Publication Data
Livesey, Anna.
Good luck / Anna Livesey.
ISBN 0-86473-459-X
I. Title.
NZ821.3—dc 21

Published with the assistance of a grant from

Printed by Astra Print, Wellington

Contents

I   Good Luck

II   Napier

III South Seas Analecta

For my family, especially Hamish,
and my teachers, especially Elaine, Alison and Chris

Acknowledgments

I would like to thank Bill Manhire, Fiona Wright, Cliff Fell, Rebecca Lovell-Smith, Hinemoana Baker, Samara McDowell, Julian Novitz, Tusiata Avia, Laura Kroetsch, John Sinclair and Jane Hurley. Also Greg O'Brien, Jenny Bornholdt, Harry Ricketts, Fergus Barrowman, Sarah Maxey, Heather McKenzie, Bub Bridger, Katherine and Justin Swift, Roger Livingstone and Gretchen Gillies. Special thanks to Chris Orsman, Elaine Lynskey, Alison Kember and my family—and extra special thanks to Hamish.

Some of these poems, or earlier versions of them, were previously published in *Sport, Glottis, Australian Journal of Canadian Studies* and *Turbine*, or as beer coasters by Propaganda, and 'Napier' was privately printed by the Pemmican Press.

1 Good Luck

'Panyassis the poet.
He is the worst pain of all.'

Acrobat Love

The strong father
whirls his son
through the air.

The mother's heart
turns somersaults.

The daughter shakes sparkles
out of every dress she owns.

Towards the Camera
for Ben

The first scene: a bar in our home town
they've been about to pull down for years.

We're ordering stout, for iron,
for good health. We're drinking to finishing

and beginning, and finishing
and beginning.

All those years
we were too young to be there—

we hoped no-one noticed us
but us.

*

In the park in your city
you point out the bats.

They are my first bats,
rolled in their wings,

hanging upside down
from the branches.

We walk under them
not touching—

things flying between us
by sonar.

*

The sound's dodgy
on this home-recording.

You play 'Ed',
a character with three lines,

two of them mouthed silently
where the synching's out.

I watched the whole video
for your shape

in the background,
for the scene where you have a drink,

the one where you cross the road
towards the camera.

Mind's Eye

I am the eye in the painting
that moves; you are the one whose gaze
slips across the paint.

From my spy hole I can see you
clear as the words in front of me—
head on one side, brows
reaching towards each other.
You're thinking about your love.

Marthe in her Bath

after Pierre Bonnard

Marthe in her bath, multi-coloured with the changing light,
floating under the jellied water. Too much of a good thing,

the label suggests—the water cure for a tubercular chest,
but she spent hours in the bath each day. No wonder

the window-frame is the dirty yellow-red of a rusting ship,
its portholes invisible above the load line of the painting.

Her breasts lie apart from each other. On the floor, tiles
like any hotel bathroom, their pattern running with the damp.

The angle of her head the saddest thing,
pushed up against a porcelain casket too small for her—

Semblance

Like the familiarity
of your story, the words

forming a shape we recognise through the particulars—
the water's stillness mirroring

stillness of last night, of two nights ago,
of before that.

The sense of recognition
when a face fits

half the considerations, almost
makes itself the same

as one you know. Take
sightings of you in the street—

several times a week, your walk, or
the curve of your head, even

a bag like the one
you used to carry.

If Happiness

If happiness is a goat with a violin,
or any such other
improbable thing,

sadness is always and only
a man with a guitar,
his fingers touching its neck,
slowly brushing its strings.

Keepsake

Given a choice
I would keep your hipbones—

your secret handles,
your body's hinge.

Child

When I think of you
I imagine your sharp eyes
finding a coin on the footpath,
the curled fist of your body
bending to pick it up, your small hand
shutting close as a purse
around it.

        You spend it
in the dairy, smiling at the woman
who swaps your windfall
for a chocolate bar.
I imagine you clicking the coin
on the counter, your face
turned up, telling her
your story about good luck.

Slippery Jack

Slimy heads of boletus
under the pines.

Fried in butter with onions,
wrapped in an omelette.

I love you like I love
their sweet slither.

Picnic

Cable Car Lookout

The oranges a pile of skins, the thermos empty,
you stand, stretch,

crumple the sandwich paper into the green council bin.
I take your hand and lead you behind the observatory.

It's a shadow-clock and you're in the middle
here at the Sundial of Human Involvement.

Byrd Memorial

I like the way you look
shovelling down hot rice—

I like the way you look
against the theatre bowl of the harbour,
against the golden set-piece of the city,
against the cloud's black curtain,
your face in the streetlight, the fork
going quickly up and down.

Home Furnishing

Things wouldn't lie about like this
if there were any justice in the world:

we would each be fitted out with matching lounge-suites,
always arrive first at our heart's desire.

The colour plates of old cookbooks show alien meals
—carrot flan, baked beetroot, glazed turbot in sauce—

but note the instructions, their collegial tone:
watch for the pages marked with a Golden Border;

here you'll turn up
a recommended Chef's Special.

*

In the furniture jungle I am attracted to oak—
the tree to stand under for protection from lightning.

On Kelburn Hill

When I told him, he was like 'oh my god', and I was like 'oh my god', and then we fell on our knees and worshipped our continuing lives, we wept a libation into the campus soil, thinking we would never lose this sense of holiness, of benediction, and the light came down on us like understanding, and we kept nothing back, but cried again, aloud, 'oh my god', and I took my pencil and scored my belief across my chest, and he took his law-text and beat the corners into his temples in an ecstasy of deliverance, and my blood ran freely over my nipples, and his blood ran freely down the sides of his face, and the ground took in our thick tears, our liquid blood, and became the very mud of our belief, the swamp of our blinding, devastating revelation.

A Ray of Human Tone

Interesting, interesting, I said.
A ray of human tone

has entered your voice—
but it was already too late.

I walked beside you
and behind you.

I called out to you,
loudly and softly.

Each time you answered,
moving your robot arms.

Each time your gestures
seemed a little less practised,

a little more rusty.
After the big melt-down

I went outside.
I saw my dog

hanging out the washing.

Afterwards

Afterwards, I went to the dairy.

Between buckets of flowers
I studied the face of a woman
who lost everything in a blaze.

I picked her up from the stack,
tucked my index finger
over her mouth,
flicked my hand
so the paper folded.

I thought how much
I love that gesture,
the one-handed paper fold—

so I did it again,
and its grainy touch
was enough to keep me happy
for ages.

Roses

Signs of botanical inspiration.
Sally Anne, Peace, Angel Wings—

floral short-hand,
growers' abbreviations.

King's Blood, Defensive,
America, and 'incognito'—

well, what would you call
the nineteenth specimen

that failed to be blue?
That one's a gimme, a crib for the cipher:

that tepid violet belongs
on a whole other plant.

Threnody

for Naomi

Wailing ode
at the time of death, today

is a good day for it.
Three years.

The sparse texture of life then.
You could walk through days

without touching the sides—a few moments
so dense it was like hewing wood.

There is nothing delicate in this,
nothing graceful, only

the cool conditional hit
of being alive.

Now the mind tucks around it
like an old blaze on a shield tree:

a diamond scored out,
the bark levered off,

fitted with a handle, painted, placed
in front of the body in battle.

The School for Sopranos

An old building,
the staircase winding up through the centre,
like the voices of the novices, circling
for a note.

Winter Mornings

They walk towards the school from the bus-stop.
None of them smoke, of course,
and they all wear scarves,
each fine-tuned throat
muffled against the cold—

but secretly they love it,
the singers in the winter.
They blow on their fingers
and watch each breath,
its silent shape on the air.

Island Bay

for Marion (and Finbar)

The sun hits the beach
at an angle that pulls the length

out of everything, laying great
shadows like fingers

from the small bubbles
of sea-weed bladders.

In the sharp sun of April
the air's got bite,

things rise above themselves,
the view goes on for miles.

Here is a place
you can watch the weather arrive—

southerlies
bullying their way north,

the unexpected cut
of the surf.

This is where
Finbar was born, in that

weather-board, glass-fronted house
like a Victorian greenhouse.

That house makes the view
cut-crystal, faceted,

offers glimpses of the island
from every window.

I think of the two of you,
watching this beach:

the sharp suck of the waves,
the air's slicing travel

into new lungs.

Fish,

gleaming,
soft as slime under those coin-thick scales.

Slit from throat to tail,
each gill a red flower, an anemone.

Eyes humanly green:
blood-veined marbles turned out with a knife.

*

Slice below the fins,
separate flesh from backbone,
wash the fish free

of blood, scales, liver, brain.
Fillets

firm as a young cheek,
a dark bloody layer,
the shining skin.

*

How surprising, the little fish
in the stomach of my big fish,

its silver body
                    swimming
against the gut wall.

Beak

*The curlew haunts the seashores and moorlands, carrying
its marks of distinction, the beak and the plaintive cry.*

Imagine me as that little bird,
legs holding me up, wings
a folded possibility, beak
investigating under stones and sometimes
opening to let out
the sound of a sad heart.

The Time of Soup

When summer acts like a fugitive animal, hiding
under the house, its tail bedraggled, its tiny body helpless,
and autumn slides past at speeds
almost invisible to the naked eye, then

comes the thick storm, the trees shaking in it,
the air a porridge of mist and water,
the roads slick—and we become

small travelling points of warmth inside
the bundles of wool, cloth, Gore-Tex, we wrap ourselves in.

This is the time of soup, when the only comfort
comes from the greased shine of pumpkin, tinned
coagulate of tomato, grains in suspension
creaming across the tongue.

Eat soup, my fellow citizens, with toast or croutons,
eat soup and survive the winter!

On the Lip

You stare down into the inverted cone
and expect the crust to be as thin
as chocolate on ice-cream, as thin as the crust
on bread, as thin as thin ice, so that
if you walk down into it you will fall
through that person-sized lid, that
Mr Burns trap-door, that green trick
the city plays on you.

You will join the beer bottles, the skateboards,
and a few of the missing persons
of the last thousand years who had the same sense of bravado,
or the same bad luck you did,
and have arrived before you.

*

There is not much to do under Mt Eden,
only discuss past lives,
only wait for someone else to arrive.

*

Everybody wishes for a Japanese tourist—
you have already spoken
every possible combination
of English and Maori
you can conjure between you.

This is a good lesson, you, the most recent arrival, think.
We should teach our children
many languages—one day
new words might be all they wish for.

Milk Wish

Mint tea in the garden.
Blue crushed glass between the roses.

When the quake struck, it was striking
to see how the ground reacted:

who stood theirs,
who jumped.

I am in contact
with the Ministry of the Interior.

They have set me to milking
three wish-fulfilling cows.

Shoeman in Love

I fell in love
through a pair of beaded slippers.

She brought them to me
to have the heels repaired.

They were black satin,
the toes hung with jet beads,

and lined with pig-skin,
a leather that absorbs sweat.

Her voice was like pig-skin
fine and strong enough

to absorb me,
but it wasn't that—

it was the taste
of the imprint of her heel

when I licked it,
holding her slipper

in front of my face
like a cup.

Last

With cautious hands
I admire the tucks
along the curves of her back,
her body's excellent design.

Milk under her skin's nap,
soft as the finest suede.
She takes me like a last,
shapes herself around me.

How did I move from her shoes to her,
from a man hooked on her secret smell
to one she allows in her bed?

The only answer is,
I don't know—
her eye fell on me,
then her body.

She pulled the blind down over the door,
turned the sign to read closed,
pushed me into the back room.
She made my body thrum
like a wire at full stretch.

Cave Country

(Te Papa)

You stand by the hill and admire the forest.
Behind you the trees mark time with their leaves.

You enter the cave between columns of mineral:
stalagmites, stalactites, their m's and t's, plaster c's and g's.

Tilt your head up for electric glow-worms,
or catch their yellow reflections in the standing water.

Around the corner, a sinkhole lets down the sky:
bones scattered in the pattern of giant birds falling.

Then what is that clatter above you on the board-walk?
It's a man with a wheelbarrow—

John Plimmer in caricature,
wheeling down to claim his corner.

In the Nature Section

Rows of butterflies
pinned behind glass.
This is the birds and bees room—
we kiss.

See, through here
half a duck disappears
into a concrete pond,

the skeletons
of two beaked whales
hang from the roof.

In a case in the next room,
folding spectacles
and a memory pad
of thin bone.

A letter begins
Dear Mother, John and I
are looking to get away

The Owl Cup

for Hamish

At the museum you lead me past tapestries and coins,
helmets and amphorae, a mummified fish,

to a case labelled 'Greek drinking cup (owl design)'.
Even behind glass, the cup's usefulness is touching:

bowl sized to fit a palm,
rim shaped for a mouth's casual grip.

It belongs on a table, or a shelf with several others,
the set taken down for each meal.

*

Standing there, I imagine the people who made it:
a man in a workshop shaping clay

to fit his hand, letting it dry to leather-hardness.
Then with a brush, black glaze, the thought of an owl,

outlining the stumpy body, wings tucked close,
the feet, and those eyes:

black circles on the terracotta,
which looked back at him and now, at us.

*

In the café we sit and drink coffee.
Under the table our feet rest together.

I think about the owl cup,
so fitly made:

the dear object, the smoothed clay that carries
a thumbprint under its rim.

II Napier

Fault

The flaw through

        the 'jewel of the bay',

its secret

        eggshell geography.

A line of uncertainty

        crossed and re-crossed

perhaps ten times
        in a morning.

Before the Quake

'Before the quake' is a phrase
still heard in Hawkes Bay:

before the quake this was all sea—
before the quake when the trams ran—
before the quake when the ships moored here—

when this creek was a river,
when the streets were narrow,
when this suburb was reclaimed from the swamp,

when we picnicked on the beach
that used to be here.

Hastings Street on the Morning of the Earthquake

Three gulls in the air,
one
        perched on the telegraph wires.
A girl in a short white dress,
a wide white hat.
A striped awning,
a mother and child,
        a gentleman
strolling to meet his bank-manager,

another man
on his way to the bakery.

        Two men on bicycles
setting out across the intersection.
In the bottom corner
        the edge of a wheel—

another cyclist, cycling
        out of the frame.

        A building
offers its facade to the camera:

        imposing
        stone,
        smooth
        pedimented cap,
        little pillars,
        recessed
        windows.

*

Overhead, a bell
mounted on the tram wires

sends its warnings
down the street.

The Ground Leapt Under Us

Darry McCarthy

Then it happened!
The ground leapt under us

like an unbroken horse,
then leapt again, over

and over and over.
When the ground

stopped jumping
and started to roll

like a ship at sea,
we sat up.

We watched
through the tumbled pines

as huge slabs of land
fell from the home paddocks

of Mohaka Station
into the sea.

W. H. Ashcroft

The wall of the Ford Garage
took on the most extraordinary
contortions:

a convulsion,
and the wall wriggled
from top to bottom
like a snake:

sometimes it bent over
and very nearly hit the Post Office.

I felt all of this was
                    happening to others,
not to me,
                    and I
was merely a spectator.

Jessie Atkinson

Alone in my father's house,
watching the piano
                    swing
across the room.

Epicentre

The shake
        equal to the detonation
of 100 million tonnes of TNT—
      slabs of rock, great

granite teeth champing each other,
          nineteen miles
under the shingle breaks

     at Aropaoanui.

Waikari Gorge

        Cars buck,
                sway—
shoot from one side of the road
     to the other,

metal and rubber's accordion flex,
        the road breaking open
           like an ice-floe.

On the *Northumberland*

Was it a sign, or some kind of joke?
A hallucination?

But we both saw it,
                    the wreck
boiling out of the harbour,

and read our ship's name

     Northumberland

on its barnacled side.

Eileen

Eileen, Eileen,
dead at nineteen,

asleep after the night shift
in a Spanish Mission building

a triumph of style that couldn't
take the pressure.

Her body, used to all-nighters,
heavy lifting, offered

only slight resistance.
Bricks, stucco, masonry, the bodies

of her colleagues who slept
on the third storey—

the building's total fragmentation,
her fall,

the ground's
rumbling reception.

Buildings

The pub tilted
        like a man after a day's work,
leaning his elbows
on the bar.
          Along the road,
            Dr Moore's hospital,

on its way to being
        fall-down drunk.

     *

In Hastings Street all
          decoration
       sheared
         off, no
      pediments, no
         chimneys, no
     roofs, no
         walls, just stumps,
      foundations,
         the buildings'
            rough tracings.

     *

At the theatre
1000 seats
      turned upside down,

the pit invaded by the audience,
the roof raised
        —and collapsed
over the stage.

Taradale

Gloucester Street, no damage
visible, only

the people crouched
outside their houses, gathered

cautiously
in the rugby field.

Soldiers

They'd seen villages after heavy shelling,
but this caught them
                                 out of uniform, not filthy
at the end of a day-long march, but in the paddock,
                    or the workshop,
                              or having smoko.

No letters from home to run a finger over,
              no head-shakes, or muttered comments:
                    the poor bloody buggers—

instead numbness and hard work
clearing the mess.

Fire

It began at the chemist's shop,
his stock flowering red
                    and silver,
sending sparks
to the neighbouring roofs.

*

Water flew in a powerful jet
to the roofs, to the top windows—

then the pressure failed.

*

When the fire took hold
it gutted the town—kindling
            chopped and laid
                    by the quake.

Fire Chief

I'm thinking of Jack,
        Grand Hotel proprietor.

Could he reach a drop in his cellar
through the long afternoon?

It was a warm day,
but he would have felt the heat
in the evening,
        heard the crackle.

He couldn't have seen it, of course,
the colour and light show

fifty feet high:

but he would have smelt it,
        smoke

        making its way
            through the gaps.

Foreshore, Evening

An over-done town picnic:
pets, furniture, make-shift beds,

                                  cooking fires.

                News or rumours
passing along the sand,

ladies asleep with their hats on.

Captain, HMS *Veronica*

I stood knee-deep in the road
as Duck and Eddie (sailors under me)
joined hands
over the trench.

The boys put themselves in the picture
to show the scale
          of the thing;

the photographer
pressed his button,
took our human wedge and stitching
into his camera.

In the background
haywire masts,
crazed paving,
the telegraph poles'
anxious lean.

Pataki

Shallow-drafted dinghies
built

for the Ahuriri lagoon—a place
of calm water,

elegant recreation.
A snap-shot, framed

through the black branches of a pine,
shows the little boats,

the cruiser
tied up at the jetty,

a few people on shore
waiting

for the pleasure-boatmen
to return.

Nine days later
the scene became

a historical document,
a relic—

a record of water
run out,

sea-floor
lifted,

small pleasures
lost,

of the pataki,
redundant,

too specialised
to cope

with the sea's
full swell.

Behind the Lens

I turned my camera
on the streets,

the crumbled walls,
the boats,

the men digging
in the rubble, but

I couldn't take
those bodies,

jerked
into history.

Two hundred
and fifty six—

I left them
their images.

Outside the school
I stood still—

two sailors
carried a stretcher

in front of me.

III South Seas Analecta

I 20,000 Fish Hooks

The Iron Age
took a long time to develop in Europe. In the Pacific
it came almost overnight: iron hoop, axes,
knives and firearms.

*

Birds of passage

Thus we called them, the traders,
flitting from rock to rock in that vast
ocean.

*

When the first ships came they were full of men.
We imagined them sailing with only each other for love.

Our old people didn't believe it—
touched them to see if any hid breasts
under those strange wraps.

They turned their noses up, though, at our sons and marvelled
at the discovery of women, our daughters.

*

100 doz. tomahawks—commencing No. 1c, 3 (common).
20 doz. tomahawks. Bright without handles.
100 doz. felling axes (common).
10 doz. clearing axes (good for use).
50 doz. Adzes (common).

5 cwt. glass beads assorted sizes and colours.
20 doz. common small scissors.
20 doz. sailors' knives.
12 pieces bright cold scarlet coarse fabric, broad.
10 dozen drawing knives.
10 dozen butchers' knives.
20,000 fish hooks assorted.
20 dozen saw files X cut & hand saw.
20 dozen Musket flints.
20 dozen Pistol flints.
5 dozen good adzes for use.

*

Other items in request
were tomahawks, axes
adzes, cloth, fish hooks,
knives and beads—large blue glass beads
were most in demand.

For bringing a log
weighing 20 to 80 pounds
from the bush to the shore, a man received
a piece of iron hoop
about five inches long.

*

For example, at the Isle of Pines, Captain Cheyne reported:
The natives could form no idea as to the use
we made of the Sandal Wood.

After seeing biscuit
they came at last to the conclusion that we ground it into Powder
and ate it.

II An Account of the Invasion of the South Pacific

Influenza broke out among the natives
and they were very much alarmed, never
having had any disease like it before.
On 8 October 1843 the death toll was 20—the next day
a large canoe full of young men approached the ship.

*

When Captain Cook
entered the Pacific in 1769

it was a virgin ocean,
pristine and savage.

Its inhabitants lived a life
of primeval innocence.

Seventy years later firearms,
alcohol and disease

had hammered away at this life
until it crumbled before them.

III Naming

They were bemused as to what sex the strangers were.
Finally, one of the sailors dropped his pants
to reveal his manhood—
a cry of recognition—

*

In Sydney the Gamaraigal's anger increased
when they realised the British were here to stay.

*

Their Ngooraialum neighbours had all got
white names, so
they took the matter up.
Several came to me daily.

In the course of a week
or two, I
christened the whole tribe, men,
women and children: Plato,
Jolly Chops, Tallyho. They
repeated their names
until they were sure of them.

*

The disease
was of a very virulent type and
after a week or so they were
unable to bury the dead.

By day and by day kept moving onwards,
leaving their dead behind them.

IV What Are We Here For?

Europeans say of themselves
that they came to do business: to trade,
to collect produce, solicit island labour.
What are we to make of the vision of a ship
that stays beyond the reef, shoots to kill,
and leaves?

*

Bêche-de-mer and copra, we push
our lips around new tongues—did we expect this place

to lay itself inside our mouths, so that we may never
be rid of the taste of it?

V First of All the Nature of Racism Must be Understood

There seems to be a certain incompatibility
between the tastes of the savage
and the pursuits of the civilised man.

This, by a process more easily marked than explained,
leads itself to the extinction of the former;
nowhere has this shown itself more visibly
than in Polynesia.

*

They die when our diseases touch them—
as if superior germs reside within our skins.
Our vices, too, they cannot contain—
alcohol, women, the pipe.

VI We Start With the Fullest Belief

One day the Christians will come
with crucifix in one hand
and dagger in the other
to cut your throats;
one day under their rule
you will be almost as unhappy as they are.

*

We start with the fullest belief in the capacity of these races;
and with the strongest conviction.
We must prevent them acquiescing
in the idea of their inferiority
inability to help themselves, etc . . .
We aim at the practical teaching of the truth.

'God hath made of one blood, etc.'

We don't aim at making Melanesians Englishmen,
but Christians; and we try to think out
the meaning and attitude of the
Melanesian mind and character—
not to suppress it but to educate it.

*

My father
was a very wicked old man. As I grew up
it seemed to be my very trade
to lie and steal, and the Sabbath I generally spent
in hunting wild pigs.

I was sick and became a Christian.

Instead of going to war I got up,
put on a decent cloth and joined a party of steady people
who were going off to remonstrate.

I am greatly delighted to add
my old erring father
seems now to be turning to the saviour too.

VII Compliant Earth

The casual poor: traits of
brutality, mistrust,
irresponsibility
and alienation.

They learned
to share their families; death
took half
before five years.

*

Europe looked to emigration
to resolve its strains, sending its unwanted children
to the four corners of the compliant earth.

*

Maklukho-Maklai

Steeped in the humanitarian and revolutionary ideals
brewing in his native Russia, he considered himself
a champion of islanders.

He collected tooth and nose size, recorded
the colour of vaginas.

Once he cut out the tongue of a servant,
cut out his tongue and larynx.

VIII Undisturbed Ownership

The tiers were piled with food—potatoes, dried
shark, eels, pork, oxen, pumpkin
and kumara.

Fine mats were displayed in piles, pound notes pinned
to pieces of string. A man
could stand between the tiers—the feast platform
was seven men tall.

The posts bore labels: Hamene—mutterings
that the feast was overdue. Takariri—we are angry
we have not provided enough.

Afterwards the tower was cut down for firewood,
and the site was never touched.

*

Beams
and rafters
painted in red
and white. The rafters
carved at the ends.

The roof raupo, the walls
totara bark,
tied with flax.
The door at the centre and at each end
a large window.

*

The island of Kapiti
was claimed by five different parties—
each declaring they had purchased it, but each
naming a different price.

In much the same way
the district of Porirua
was claimed by eight separate parties,
each claiming Te Rauparaha had sold it to them,
each claiming the chief had offered
the undisturbed ownership of these lands
to him
alone.

*

A Mr Webster, an
American, claims to have purchased
40 miles of frontage
on the west side of the River Piako;
a Mr Painham claims nearly the whole
of the north coast
of the Northern Island;
a Mr Wentworth, of
New South Wales, asserts his right to 20,100,000 acres
in the Middle Island;

Catlin & Co. to 7,000,000;
Weller & Co. to 3,557,000;
Jones & Co. to 1,930,000;
Peacock & Co. to 1,450,000;
Green & Co. to 1,377,000;
Guard & Co. to 1,200,000;
and the New Zealand Company, 20,000,000.

IX In the Far-Off Places

The missionaries have been successful, but
at present they are cultivating their land.

To use the words of Rev.
Henry Williams—
they are just holding on for their children, seeing
no better prospect.

They cannot send them home to England—
it is too expensive.

New South Wales would not be desirable for them,
and this
is their only chance—

*

There is only one thing
which keeps husband and wife together
in the far-off places:
only one lack that separates them—

love,
and the want of it.

X Bait

As usual with functions where Britons are concerned
the event concluded with a feast.

The Europeans were regaled with a cold luncheon
at Mr Busby's house.

The Maoris, on the lawn,
had pork, potatoes and Kororiroi:

a mixture of flour, water and sugar
of which they are immensely fond.

These delicacies they devoured
sans knives, *sans* forks.

*

Blankets were brought by Mr Williams.
These I call the bait.

The fish did not know
there was a hook within.
He took the bait and was caught.

When he came to a chief, Mr Williams presented his hook,
and drew out a subject for the Queen.

XI Sugars, Cinnamons and Sweets

Europeans were expensive to maintain
at the princely level
to which they were accustomed.

They were notoriously susceptible
to disease
& alcoholism
& allergic to hard work.

*

If the Quashee refuses to do what work the maker intended:
bringing out these various sugars, cinnamons, and sweets
of the West-Indian Islands
for the benefit of all mankind, well then,
neither will the Powers permit Quashee
to continue growing pumpkins there
for his own lazy benefit.

XII These Alsatian Days

Dark
as the history of New Zealand was
during these Alsatian days,
there is no chapter
quite so dark
as the story of the seagoing natives:

taken
from these sunny shores, abandoned
in foreign countries, driven
at the end of the lash
to tasks beyond their strength.

The result:
many died, but undying
was the hate of the poisoned
souls of the survivors

*

Still
the Maori
were a numerous, virile
and warlike race,
capable of deeds
of blackest barbarism,
but equally adaptable
to the softening influences
of Christianity
& Civilisation.

*

All Transylvanians are lazy, all
Calathumpians unintelligent or
all Pantagonians violent.

So we are freed
from the tedious need
to make individual judgements.

XIII The Roaring of the Sea

O Potatau
you will be a father to us,
will you not?
A great cheering and
a salute was fired.

The noise was like the roaring of the sea.

*

We saw that the elder brother
was quarrelling with the younger;
so one man was appointed
to suppress the fighting and stop the blood.

He is Te Wherowhero:
Potatau, King.

XIV This is Our Thought

We heard that Taranaki was destroyed.
Afterwards came news about Ngatiruanui;
here we were perplexed.

We had not heard there was fighting
until the soldiers had gone aboard the ships:
then we heard.

Now this offence was from the Pakeha:
hence, we said,
we are strangers to one another.

This is our thought;
we are divided,
you on one side,
we on the other.

*

This is another thing, about the roads.

The roads are not simply for fetching food
from a man's farm;
throughout the island, it is this
that creates fear.

At Taranaki, the road being there,
your guns reached the pa.

*

I have not heard that the roads
are stopped up;
the great road of the Waikato
is not stopped, the road
of the Waipa river
is not stopped. The Pakehas
and the Maoris
are travelling upon them;

the road of the Union Jack
alone is closed.

XV Argonauts of the Western Pacific

Noa Noa

I was sad; shall I manage to recover
any trace of the past, so remote, so
mysterious?

The present has nothing to say to me:
to get back to the ancient hearth, to revive the fire
in the midst of all these ashes.

*

Ethnology is in a sadly
ludicrous, not to say tragic,
position. At the very moment
when it begins to put its workshop in order,
to forge its proper tools,
to start, ready for work,
on its appointed task,
the material of its study
melts away.

Just now, when
the aims and methods
of the scientific field
ethnology
have taken shape,
when men fully trained for the work
have begun to travel
into savage countries
and study their inhabitants—these die away
under our very eyes.

*

Eve
after the fall, still able to walk naked without shame,
preserving her animal beauty
as at the first day.

Like Eve's her body is still that of an animal—
but her head has progressed, her mind developed subtlety; love
has imprinted an ironical smile upon her lips.

XVI Cane

I saw Wallace
hit Berracone with hand
on face and nose—
blood run out.

There was fire on the floor—
Wallace put Berracone foot in fire
and fire burn Berracone.

Berracone, he sick man then.

*

In their huts men from Malaita, Makira,
men whose homes are Vanuatu,
Guadalcanal, men
are sleeping.

They are the black
of a Queensland night.

In their huts, their noises of sleep
are the whine of a mosquito,
the sweet
drip
of sugar cane.

*

What did they come for,
to this land of sugar
and flour?

The days are long—long
as the light lasts. The cane
rises and falls with the years.

In the black of their huts
they grease firearms, test
the edge to a knife.

*

Hungary killed himself in 1877,
having been observed attempting to starve himself.

He had been depressed and fretted.
His two brothers, engaged with him,
had both died.

Jack hanged himself at his place of abode.
Jack had been sullen for some time.
He said the men from the village of his enemies
chaffed him.

The manager of Richmond Plantation at Mackay
discovered the body of Nungarooarlu
hanging by a fishing line on an acacia tree.

Semen, a servant at Innisfail,
attempted to kill himself while incarcerated,
but only succeeded in self-
castration.

*

Remember Queensland—
remember Kalah?

Kalah of Api Island
was murdered with an axe
by two men from Santo.

*

He returns to the bay he came from.

From the back his buttocks
kiss the ship goodbye.

On his shoulder his breech-
loading rifle, on
his face—
on his face, from here,
who can say?

XVII An Act to Make Provision

How is it possible
to make a man go into the box
and admit he is the father
of a half-caste child?

I do not think that is a nice, or proper, or fair
thing to do.

A half-caste may belong to a syndicate
and it is hard to tell who the father is.

*

The size of the head
and its bumps
represent the shape
and size
of the brain within.

Aboriginal skulls reveal deficiencies in
moral and intellectual organs
and excesses in the passions, aggression
and the observational instinct.

*

If Australia is to be a country
fit for our children and their children to live in, we must
KEEP THE BREED PURE.

The half-caste inherits the vices of both
and the virtues of neither.

Do you want Australia
to be a community of mongrels?

I would rather see
my daughter dead than kissing a black man

or nursing a little coffee-coloured brat
she was mother to.

*

Elections Act 1850
Master and Servants Act 1861
Industrial and Reformatory Schools Act 1865
Polynesian Labourers Act 1868
Pacific Islanders Protection Act 1872
Pacific Islanders Protection Act 1875
Pacific Island Labourers Act 1880
Pearl-Shell and Bêche-de-mer Fishery Act 1881
Native Labourers Protection Act 1884
Oaths Act Amendment Act 1884
Aboriginals Protection and Restriction of the Sale of Opium
    Act 1897
Pacific Island Labourers Act 1901
Post and Telegraph Act 1901
Immigration Restriction Act 1901
Sugar Bounty Act 1903
Aborigines Act 1905
Bounties Act 1907
Northern Territory Aboriginals Act 1910
Aborigines Act 1911
White Women's Protection Ordinance 1926
Commonwealth Electoral Act 1962
Royal Commission Into Aboriginal Deaths in Custody 1991
Native Title Act 1993

XVIII She Is Not

She is not an
'aboriginal'
while so employed.

But
whenever any such half-caste
returns to her people
and resides with them,
she becomes an
'aboriginal'
within the meaning of the Act.

*

Upon report by the Protector
that venereal or contagious
or infectious diseases
prevail among the aboriginals
of any locality,
the Commissioner of Police
may cause all affected
to be mustered
and removed

to some island or other place appointed for the purpose
to be there detained until cured.

*

Well Mither . . . all black-fellow gone!
All this my country!
Little Pickaninny, I

run about here.
Corroboree; great fight;
all canoe about. Only
me now Mither.

All this
my country.

*

to search Aborigines
their dwellings and belongings at any time
to confiscate Aboriginal property
read Aboriginal mail
confine Aboriginal children
expel Aborigines
far from their families
order medical inspections
and prohibit dancing

XIX Notes by a Papuan Judge

Murder in their eyes
is not a crime at all; sometimes
it is a duty, sometimes
a social etiquette, sometimes
a relaxation.

*

You think how many kanakas
learned good agricultural practice
from planters, how many
got seed coconuts
from us if they wanted them.

And you think
how many were taught things—driving trucks
and cars, mechanics' jobs,
carpentry, plumbing.

*

On a Monday morning,
we all woke up
to servantless houses.

The man from the German club
was so obese
he was unable to put his own shoes on.

He stood in the road,
waving his shoes
and pleading with passers-by
to help him.

The strikers
moved through the town—
to the Anglican
or to the Catholic church.

The strike leaders were beaten
for confessions; kept below decks
in a sweltering hulk.

They were made to stand on deck
until they collapsed,
their skins
bubbling.

XX Masai Ariana

Gov. Murray, 1861-1940

However, I do not suppose
it matters much—
the Japanese will have not only Papua
and New Guinea, but
Australia and New Zealand
in another fifty
years.

Thank God, I
shall be dead.

*

Aristocratic, autocratic, Labor-
inclined, witty,
intellectual & athletic,
Catholic,
married &
alone, kind
& responsive
to the Papuan people,
elderly &
attractive to women. A
misfit
in his own society, he
found his kingdom
in someone
else's.

*

For forty days and nights
watch fires burnt
on the hills around the town.

On the forty-first day
thousands of Papuans arrived in Hanuabada
for the death feast.

They lined the hills.

They sat in silence;
the only sound the tapping
of a thousand native drums.

*

3 February 1942

The first bombs fell
on Moresby.

Fires, fires
and fires on the hills.

Look Murray,
the Japanese.

Notes

I   Good Luck

'Threnody': 'shield trees' are trees which have had a piece of bark cut out to be used as a shield. The tree continues to grow and the blaze remains visible on the trunk. This is a traditional Aboriginal way of making shields.

'Marthe in her Bath' is based on *Bath (1925)* by Pierre Bonnard. His wife Marthe suffered from tuberculosis for many years.

II   Napier

Most of the factual material for this sequence was gathered from *Quake: Hawke's Bay 1931*, by Matthew Wright, published by Reed, Auckland, 2001.

'Before the Quake' is adapted from Matthew Wright.

'The Ground Leapt Under Us': the first two quotes are almost verbatim from Darry McCarthy (a school-girl) and W.H. Ashcroft, a man working in Napier. The third 'quote' is based on Jesse Atkinson's experience.

'On the *Northumberland*' records the experience of cadet A.F.R. Irwin and others on the freighter *Northumberland,* which was at Port Ahuriri when the quake struck. The wreck they saw rising up from the sea-floor was another *Northumberland*, wrecked off Napier in May 1887.

'Eileen' commemorates the death of Eileen Williams, one of the eight nurses killed when the new nurses' home collapsed. The building had not been properly earthquake strengthened.

'Captain, HMS *Veronica*' is based on an extant photograph, (see http://www.directenergy.com.au/FamilyTrees/napier_earthquake_1931_photo_gal.htm), but the characters in it are fictional.

'Pataki': pataki were small, flat-bottomed boats with retractable centre-boards, developed for use in the lagoon. The earthquake raised the sea-floor and drained most of the lagoon, leaving nowhere for the pataki to be used.

III South Seas Analecta

'South Seas Analecta' was written—or perhaps more accurately collected —in 1999 when I was doing *History 111: Colonial Encounters, Pacific Experiences* at Victoria University. I didn't plan to write a poem, but, one day quite early on in the course, I found something in the readings that I didn't want to let go—so I copied it out. And then I found something else, and something else, and then I started making bits up and changing things around. It wasn't until about a year later that I sat down and sorted everything out to create the finished poem.

While I changed things, and made some things up, many of the words in the poem aren't mine. I've borrowed and reset them. And, because I hadn't imagined the end product when I started (and because it's a poem, not a scholarly text), I didn't keep notes on where I got each piece from. A very abbreviated and patchy bibliography, compiled years after the fact, follows below. It does not include all, or even most of the sources I used, but it gives some idea of the range. I hope 'South Seas Analecta' resets the found elements in a way that is both respectful and challenging. I owe a large debt to all the people who created the resources I plundered and to Giselle Byrnes, Paul D'Arcy and Kate Hunter who taught the course.

Judith Basset, Judith Binney, and Eric Olsen, *The People and the Land/ Te Tangata me Te Whenua: An Illustrated History of New Zealand, 1820-1920,* Wellington, 1990.

James Belich, *Making Peoples,* Auckland, 1996.

B. Gammage, 'The Rabaul Strike, 1929', *JPH*, vol. 10, (3), 1975, pp.3-29.

W.J. Gardner and W.D. McIntyre (eds.), *Speeches and Documents in New Zealand History,* Oxford, 1971.

Kerry Howe, 'Firearms and indigenous warfare: a case study', *JPH*, 9, 1974, 21-38.

Amanda Morgan, 'Mystery in the Eye of the Beholder: Cross Cultural Encounters on 19th Century Yap,' *Journal of Pacific History,* 31, 1, June 1996, 27-41.

William Renwick (ed), *Sovereignty and Indigenous Rights,* Wellington, 1991.

Henry Reynolds, *The Law of the Land,* Ringwood, 1987.

Kay Saunders, '"Troublesome Servants": The strategies of Resistance employed by Melanesian indentured labourers on plantations in colonial Queensland', *JPH*, 14, 1979, 168-183.

Dorothy Shineberg, 'The Sandalwood Trade in Melanesian Economics, 1841-65', *JPH*, 1, 1966, 129-146.

Ranginui Walker, *Ka Whawhai Tonu Matou Struggle Without End,* Auckland, 1990.